NEAR-DEATH EXPERIENCES AND REINCARNATION

IN HISTORY

ENZO GEORGE

rosen publishing's
rosen
central®

New York

Published in 2020 by The Rosen Publishing Group, Inc.
29 East 21st Street
New York, NY 10010

Produced for Rosen by Calcium Creative Ltd
Editors for Calcium: Sarah Eason and Harriet McGregor
Designer: Paul Myerscough and Jessica Moon
Picture researcher: Rachel Blount

Photo credits: Cover: Shutterstock: Juergen Faelchle; Inside: Library of
Congress: p. 27; George Grantham Bain Collection: p. 26; Shutterstock:
Zvonimir Atletic: p. 17; Salvador Aznar: p. 43; BasPhoto: p. 6; Ronnie Chua:
pp. 32–33; Graham De'ath: p. 19; Gaetan-L: p. 29; Jorisvo: p. 21; Jacob Lund:
p. 30; Masarik: p. 4; Hoika Mikhail: pp. 3, 8; Huey Min: p. 37; Ruben Pinto:
p. 36; Stephen Rees: p 16; Bruce Rolff: p. 28; Saiko3p: p. 11; Sezer66: pp. 1,
31; Darko Sikman: p. 12; StockPhotosArt: p 5; Theskaman306: p. 10; Thoom:
p. 7; Vaflya: p. 20; WillemA: p. 40; Wikimedia Commons: pp. 22–23; Pedro
Berruguete: p. 14; Workshop of Master of Boucicaut: p. 15; Miss Carter: p. 24;
Giovanni Dall'Orto: p. 9; Detroit Publishing Co.: p. 41; Max Halberstadt: p. 34;
B. McClellan/Kurz & Allison: pp. 38–39; NASA/Apollo 17 crew; taken by either
Harrison Schmitt or Ron Evans: p. 35; Schäfer, Johann: p. 25; Signal Corps:
p. 42; Newell Convers Wyeth: p. 1.

Cataloging-in-Publication Data

Names: George, Enzo.
Title: Near-death experiences and reincarnation in history / Enzo George.
Description: New York : Rosen Central, 2020. | Series: The paranormal
throughout history | Includes glossary and index.
Identifiers: ISBN 9781725346659 (pbk.) | ISBN 9781725346598 (library bound)
Subjects: LCSH: Near-death experiences—Juvenile literature. |
Reincarnation—Juvenile literature.
Classification: LCC BF1045.N4 G47 2020 | DDC 133.901'3—dc23

Manufactured in the United States of America

Cover: Throughout the ages, people have claimed that the spirit leaves the
body after death and passes into another realm.

CONTENTS

CHAPTER 1

BORN AGAIN

One of the great mysteries about human life is what happens when we die. Since earliest times, people have believed that the soul may survive in some form or another after the body dies. Some peoples argued that the dead haunted Earth as ghosts, or went to an afterlife. Others believed that the souls of the dead passed into new bodies and were born again on Earth. This process is known as reincarnation.

Ancient peoples disposed of dead bodies carefully in the belief that their owners might still need them.

Body and Soul

Reincarnation is based on the idea that the body and soul are separate. This belief was at the core of funeral rituals held in ancient societies such as Mesopotamia and Egypt. Ancient peoples believed that dead bodies had to be carefully buried, burned, or preserved so that the souls of the dead could survive in the afterlife. Early religions were based on the idea of keeping the gods happy—including the gods of the dead.

Cycles of Life

In South Asia and other parts of the world, life was based on farming. Peoples who observed the regular cycle of birth, death, and rebirth in their seeds and crops also wondered whether there might be a cycle that involved humans coming back to life after death. No one knows when a belief in reincarnation began, but it was probably among the ancient faiths of South Asia. These beliefs became the basis of later religions such as Hinduism and Jainism. In the 600s BCE, they were incorporated as a key belief of the Buddhist faith. Hindus, Jains, and Buddhists taught that the soul is reincarnated and goes through numerous lives until it attains a state of spiritual enlightenment, which in Buddhism is called nirvana.

A belief in reincarnation is also said to have appeared among the ancient Greeks and among the Celts, who lived in Europe from the 700s BCE. The belief may originally come from South Asia, or it may have arisen independently among farming peoples who also saw human life as an echo of the cycles of the seasons.

By about 3500 BCE, people in northern Europe were using stones to build tombs called dolmens to mark the graves of important individuals.

WHAT IS DEATH?

For many ancient peoples, death was a state that resembled life. The Egyptians buried wealthy people with belongings to take to the afterlife. One purpose of disposing of a dead body correctly was to ensure that the spirits of the dead would not return to haunt the living.

Common Ideas

One common religious idea shared by many ancient peoples from Europe to Asia was that the body and soul were different things. The body was physical and therefore could grow old and weak. The spiritual soul, however, did not decay: it remained perfect.

Another common belief was that the boundary between life and death could be crossed in both directions. The spirits of the dead went to the afterlife, which could be either enjoyable or unpleasant, but some returned to reappear on Earth as ghosts. Some people who had come close to death, such as from disease or from wounds received in battle, reported meeting dead relatives or other spirits in the afterlife.

This carving shows the boat that the Egyptians believed carried the dead to the afterlife.

Ancient Greece

Another way that the dead could return to life was by inhabiting new bodies. From about the 500s BCE, ancient Greek philosophers, or thinkers, discussed the idea that the soul might last forever. In that case, the philosopher Plato reasoned, souls must pass from one physical body to another. He argued that there must be a place where dead souls gathered after they died, while they waited to be born into new bodies. When Plato described the death of his teacher, the philosopher Socrates, he noted that Socrates said "the living spring from the dead."

Followers of the Orphic religion in Greece believed that the soul was immortal and longed to be free, while the body held it prisoner. A belief in reincarnation was also common among the ancient Romans, who ruled much of Europe from the first century BCE.

While some peoples believed the dead traveled underground, others believed they went to the sky.

The End of Reincarnation

In the first century CE, a new faith began to spread in the Roman Empire. Christianity taught that people who lived a good life were rewarded by their souls spending eternity in paradise, while the bad went to hell. These teachings allowed no room for the idea of reincarnation. As Christianity spread, the belief in reincarnation died out in the West.

A GREEK WARRIOR

In the ancient Greek poem *The Odyssey*, written by Homer in about the eighth century BCE, Odysseus visits the underworld, which is ruled by the god Hades. Odysseus meets the ghost of the hero Achilles. Achilles tells him that he would prefer to be the poorest peasant on Earth than lord of the whole underworld.

The Greeks believed the dead could live on by ensuring that people remembered them after their deaths. They left gifts at tombs and told stories of famous warriors and how they bravely met their deaths. Their spirits left their bodies at the moment of death and traveled to the underworld.

A Warrior's Story

In the fourth century BCE, the famous philosopher Plato recorded a story showing that the soul was constantly reincarnated. His account tells how the warrior Er was killed and lay on a battlefield for ten days until the bodies of the dead were collected at the end of the fighting. Just as Er's body was about to be cremated, or burned, the warrior came back to life.

Warriors such as Hector and Achilles, shown on the detail of this vase, were thought to live on after death.

8

The Afterlife

Er said that he had traveled to the afterlife, where he watched the souls of the dead being sorted into two groups. Those who had lived good lives were sent into the sky, to a pleasant, refreshing place. Those who had lived bad lives were sent down into the ground to a place of misery. They could only escape by suffering 10 times the suffering they had caused to others in life.

Er also watched souls being prepared for reincarnation by choosing what their next life would be. He said that many people chose to become animals, believing animals had easier lives than people. The souls then drank from a river that caused forgetfulness, so that when they were reborn they would remember nothing of their former lives.

This Roman mosaic shows the Greek musician Orpheus charming wild animals by playing his harp-like lyre.

Return from the Underworld

Many ancient peoples told myths about people who visited the underworld and returned. In Sumer, it was the hero Gilgamesh, while in Egyptian stories it was the god Osiris. In Greek myths, both Odysseus and the hero Aeneas visit the underworld to gain advice from the dead. In one famous story, the musician Orpheus descends to the underworld to rescue his wife, Eurydice. When Orpheus breaks his promise not to look back at Eurydice before they reach the upper world, his wife vanishes forever.

9

CHAPTER 2

REINCARNATION AND RELIGION

Ideas about death are central to most faiths. People use religion to give meaning to life, which includes what happens after death. In Christianity, for example, the soul goes either to heaven or hell, depending on whether a person has lived well or badly. Islam also teaches that the soul lives only once.

This Indian girl is reading a Hindu text next to the Ganges River. Hindus began to believe in reincarnation around 3,000 years ago.

Some religions are based on the idea that existence needs reincarnation. Theologists, or people who study religions, believe this reflects the association people made between human life, death, and rebirth and the cycle of seeds growing into plants, which die in winter before giving rise to new plants in spring.

Vedic Religions

In parts of India, the ideas of what became the Hindu religion were recorded between about 1500 and 500 BCE in texts known as the Vedas. These early mentions of reincarnation, developed over centuries, were based on two central ideas. One idea was rebirth, when the immortal soul passed either to heaven or hell, or into a new body on Earth. The other was karma, which was the idea that reincarnation was part of a system of spiritual reward or punishment. The good people did during their lives would be reflected by reincarnation on a more enjoyable level of society. Those who had committed evil acts were punished with a more miserable existence. Reincarnation is a constant cycle from which the soul can escape only if a person embarks on a journey of spiritual enlightenment that frees it from the cycle and allows it to reach heaven. Hindu texts such as the Upanishads teach people how they can liberate themselves from the cycle of reincarnation.

Reincarnation and Buddha

In Buddhism, which began in northern India in the 500s BCE, reincarnation took another form. Gautama Buddha, who created the religion, taught that the soul was not immortal because nothing was permanent. On death, the soul dissolved to become part of everything else in the universe. It could later be reincarnated into another body, but not directly as in Hinduism.

This statue in northern India marks the place where Buddha is said to have achieved spiritual enlightenment.

HUNT FOR THE DALAI LAMA

In the seventh century, the Buddhist faith that had begun hundreds of years earlier in northern India reached Tibet, a mountainous region in the foothills of the Himalayas. Tibetans became enthusiastic Buddhists, and over time they developed a distinctive type of Buddhism with its own teachings and its own spiritual leader, named the Dalai Lama. Reincarnation was a key belief for all Buddhists, but in Tibet it became of central importance.

Tenzin Gyatso was born to a poor Tibetan family in 1935. He became the 14th Dalai Lama in 1940.

An Unbroken Chain

In the 1400s, Tibetan Buddhists came to believe that each Dalai Lama was a reincarnation of all the Dalai Lamas who had gone before. The spirit moved from one body to the next. Therefore, Buddhist monks began a tradition of seeking out a new leader each time a Dalai Lama died. Since the 1400s, they believe, there has been an unbroken series of 14 Dalai Lamas.

A Political Problem

Tibet is coming increasingly under control of its huge neighbor, China. The Tibetans dislike Chinese influence, and see the Dalai Lama as a symbol of resistance. The current Dalai Lama, Tenzin Gyatso, has said that he will not be reborn in Tibet if it is under Chinese control. The Chinese government, meanwhile, is making signals that it intends to be involved in the search to find the next Dalai Lama. Tibetans fear the Chinese will try to create a Dalai Lama who is friendly toward China.

Finding the new leader is the job of the High Lamas, or senior priests, and the government of Tibet. They can spend up to four years searching in Tibet for children who were born at the same time the old Dalai Lama died. The priests examine their dreams and visions for clues of where to look, and also follow signs such as the direction the smoke blows when the old Dalai Lama's body is cremated. They also visit a sacred lake in central Tibet, Lhamo La-tso, to seek clues from the lake's guardian spirit, Palden Lhamo. She is said to have promised the first Dalai Lama that she would help find his successors.

Identifying the Lama

When they find a child who is a possible candidate, the priests use a series of tests to find out if he is the right person. The tests include showing the child various objects to see if he can recognize possessions that belonged to the old Dalai Lama. In this way, the priests come up with a single candidate. If more than one boy fulfils the requirements, the priests draw lots to pick an individual. The boy then enters a monastery to begin his training to become the spiritual leader of Tibet.

MEDIEVAL RELIGION

In the Middle Ages, the Catholic Church fought to defend its beliefs. It launched holy wars called crusades against the Muslims of the Middle East. In Europe, it also went to war with Christians whose beliefs were different from Catholic teachings, including those who believed in reincarnation.

This painting illustrates a story in which Cathar texts burned in a fire while Catholic texts did not. The Church claimed that this proved that Cathar beliefs were wrong.

The Cathars

In the 1100s, a new Christian group appeared that had different beliefs from those of the Catholic Church. These were the Cathars of southern France and northern Italy, who are also known as Albigensians, after the French city of Albi. The Cathars were influenced by ideas from Persia and the Middle East. They believed there were two gods, one good and one evil. The evil god created the physical world, including human beings themselves. The Cathars believed this world was evil and full of sin. The good god created human souls, which the Cathars believed were the spirits of angels trapped inside bodies created by the evil god. These spirits were immortal, so they were reincarnated again and again, until they could escape and enter heaven by performing Cathar rituals.

Crusade in France

The Catholic Church rejected this teaching. It said there was one god, and that souls were not reincarnated. In 1208, the pope, the head of the Catholic Church, sent a messenger to the Cathars. The messenger was killed, and the pope called on Catholics to begin a crusade, or religious war, against the Cathars.

For 20 years, the Cathars and their allies fought armies from northern France. In 1209, crusaders massacred more than 7,000 Cathars and Catholics in the city of Béziers. In 1229, the war was ended by the Treaty of Paris, but the Cathars continued to preach their faith.

Harsh Punishment

The Church set up a religious court called the Inquisition to punish the Cathars for heresy, or false beliefs. Over the next century, hundreds of Cathars were put on trial. Most were hanged or burned at the stake. In one punishment, more than 200 Cathars were burned at the same time. By about 1330, the Church had finally managed to get rid of the Cathar faith completely.

In this illustration, Crusaders are driving Cathars from the French city of Carcassone in 1209.

CHAPTER 3
SLEEPING HEROES

Some reincarnation stories tell of heroes who come back to life after a long death-like sleep. These heroes are often great leaders or warriors who become a symbol of a people or a nation. They are said to be waiting in a hidden place for a sign that their people need them. These stories appear around the world.

Sir Francis Drake is said to be ready to come to England's aid if someone bangs on his old military drum.

Heroes in Wait

In many versions of the story, the hero is a ruler who is said to have taken shelter in a mountain cave somewhere in his former lands. Other locations where the hero waits include remote islands and a parallel world that is invisible to humans.

The hero is often dressed in armor and is surrounded by his armed knights. Sometimes the hero is waiting for a sign, such as a hunting horn being blown or a drum being played. At other times, the hero wakes from time to time and looks out from his hiding place for certain signs that all is well.

Heroes of the Nation

Most sleeping heroes will help their countrymen at the time of their greatest peril. St. Wenceslas of Bohemia in the Czech Republic is said to sleep in a mound with a huge army, and will return on his white horse, carrying a magical sword. King Sebastian I of Portugal is said to be waiting to return on a hazy, misty morning. Ogier the Dane was a warrior of the ninth century who will return to save Denmark, while Vytautas the Great will rise from his tomb to fight a huge battle to aid Lithuania. Frederick Barbarossa, the Holy Roman Emperor, sleeps in a mountain, ready to defend his empire.

Constantine the Great, who ruled the Byzantine Empire, is said to have been turned into a stone statue, in which form he waits to help his people.

There are also religious sleeping heroes. They include the Hidden Imam, or Islamic leader, who is said to be ready to accompany Jesus back to Earth. Some Buddhist monks are said to preserve themselves as mummies so they can come back to life when Buddha returns to Earth.

It is said that Saint John the Evangelist will rise from his grave to defeat the Antichrist.

17

KING ARTHUR

One of the most famous sleeping heroes is the legendary English king Arthur. He is said to have ruled with his queen, Guinevere, from his castle at Camelot in the sixth century CE. Arthur is most famous for gathering a group of knights, such as Sir Gawain and Sir Lancelot, who carried out many brave quests.

In this illustration, King Arthur receives the magical sword Excalibur from the Lady of the Lake.

The figure of Arthur may have been based on a real ruler who led English resistance against Germanic invaders, such as the Angles and the Saxons, but his story soon became mixed up with legends about magic. It was said that he inherited his kingdom because he was the only person who could pull a magical sword from a stone where it was mysteriously stuck. When Arthur was killed in battle, it was said that his body was put on a boat to float to the mysterious island of Avalon. Avalon was said to be a magical place ruled by nine sorceress sisters, where the land produced everything people needed to live long and healthy lives.

The Sleeping King

In the 1100s, a writer named Geoffrey of Monmouth wrote a version of the story of Arthur in which the king did not die at all. Instead, his badly wounded body was sent to Avalon, to be healed and to allow Arthur to rest. In this story, Arthur is the "once and future king."

He waits to be summoned to help his people in their time of crisis. Over the centuries, a number of stories were told about people who stumbled across lost caves, where they found the king sleeping with the sword Excalibur by his side, or where they found the Knights of the Round Table and Queen Guinivere sleeping while they waited for Arthur's return from Avalon.

Arthurian Places

Historians identify the Isle of Avalon with Glastonbury in Somerset, in southern England. Many other places are also associated with Arthur, including Tintagel, a rocky island in Cornwall, England, that is often believed to have been the location of Camelot. The cathedral at the town of Winchester has a copy of the Round Table, and people have claimed that the town was once the site of Camelot.

Arthur and his knights sat at a round table, so that none appeared more important than the rest.

A Pueblo God

Sleeping heroes similar to King Arthur appear in cultures around the world. The Pueblo of Arizona and other neighboring peoples believed that they were once ruled by a divine god-ruler named Montezuma. They claim that Montezuma sleeps inside a mountain in the state and will one day return to save them. In Colorado, Sleeping Ute Mountain is said to contain a warrior god recovering from wounds received in a great battle against evil.

A GERMAN HERO

The Holy Roman Emperor Charlemagne is said to lie beneath the Untersberg Mountain near Salzburg in Austria, where he is cared for by dwarfs. He wakes from his sleep every 100 years to check that ravens are still flying around the mountain. Once he has confirmed this sign that all is well, he goes back to his slumbers.

The Untersberg Mountain rises above the city of Salzburg. It is part of the Alps mountain chain.

King of the Franks

Charlemagne was king of the Franks, who lived in what is roughly now France and Germany. In 800, the Pope crowned him emperor of the Holy Roman Empire, which united much of Europe for the first time since the days of ancient Rome centuries earlier. Charlemagne encouraged a period of great learning and artistic achievement, and was a great supporter of the Roman Catholic Church.

Inside the Mountain

Charlemagne died in 814 and was buried in his capital at Aachen, now in Germany. Rumors soon began that he was not dead. Instead, people said that he sat in a trance inside Untersberg Mountain. The king is surrounded by his knights, with a crown on his head and his sceptre —a rod that was a symbol of authority—in his hand. His beard has grown so that it covers the breastplate of his armor and has wrapped itself twice around the table at which he sits. According to one version of the story, when the beard reaches the last corner of the table for the third time, the king will awake. This is a sign that the last days of Earth have arrived, and that Judgment Day, as described in the Bible, is about to begin.

This church window has a portrait of Charlemagne to celebrate his support of the Catholic Church.

Variations on the Myth

In some versions of the Charlemagne story, he sleeps at the bottom of a deep well inside the castle at Nuremberg in Germany. In other versions, the sleeping king is not Charlemagne at all. Instead, it is Frederick Barbarossa, who was the Holy Roman Emperor from 1155 to 1190. He is said to sleep inside Kyffhäuser Mountain in central Germany, where he awaits Judgment Day.

21

CHAPTER 4
A SCIENTIFIC PERSPECTIVE

By the early 1800s, death had become the subject of serious study. The famous French chemist Antoine Lavoisier carried out a unique experiment on his own death.

Death by Guillotine

Lavoisier was an aristocrat who had worked for the French government, which was overthrown in 1789 by a revolution. For a few years, Lavoisier kept working, but his enemies among the revolutionaries eventually had him put on trial and sentenced to death by guillotine in 1794. This was a large sliding blade that cut off the head from its victim. Lavoisier arranged for his assistant to stand next to the guillotine, and to pick up his head as soon as it was sliced off. Lavoisier would give a sign if he was aware of the world around him. It was said that when the man picked up the head, it blinked every second for 15 or 20 seconds.

Most people say the story is made up. There are many stories of criminals who also arranged to make signals after their executions, but none ever succeeded. Meanwhile, doctors were carefully examining human bodies to learn about death.

New Ideas

Another view of death was held by the Transcendentalists in the United States. This was a group of writers and thinkers that developed in the 1830s. They were fascinated by Eastern beliefs such as Hinduism, which were little known in the West. The Transcendentalists believed all of nature, including humans, was joined in one whole.

During the French Revolution, executioners displayed the heads of those who had just been killed.

The Transcendentalists believed in a soul that existed before it took possession of a body. That suggested it must also exist after its body dies, which led them to accept that reincarnation was a fact. The writer Henry David Thoreau studied nature closely. He observed: "The hawk that soars so loftily and circles so steadily and apparently without effort, has earned this power by faithfully creeping on the ground as a reptile in a former state of existence."

RESEARCHING DEATH

Since the early scientific age, death has continued to attract the attentions of leading thinkers. The subject brings together not only the study of the body, but also the way in which the mind works, together with ideas about the soul and the nature of religious belief.

Among those who investigated death was the philosopher William James, shown here interviewing a medium.

The Unique Soul

In the early 1700s, the Swedish inventor and scientist Emanuel Swedenborg became increasingly fascinated by spiritual questions. He approached them in the same kind of analytical way he had studied technological problems. In the 1740s, he claimed to have had a religious vision that enabled him to move easily between life and death, where he visited heaven and hell and talked to angels and other spirits. Swedenborg came to believe that death was like an extension of life, in which the spirit survived and continued to develop. He believed, however, that reincarnation was not possible. Each soul was unique, he argued, and the idea that it could pass from person to person was "absurd."

Shared Consciousness

In the early 1800s, the German philosopher Arthur Schopenhauer also began to question the nature of death. For Schopenhauer, there was no such thing as an independent, physical world that could be directly experienced by individuals. Schopenhauer said that people constructed their own versions of the world and then responded to them as if they were reality. This included death itself, which people see and describe in a particular way. Although Schopenhauer says life and death are clearly different, he also says we see death as the opposite of life because we teach ourselves to do so. In contrast, he argues that in some ways death can be seen as the point of life, because everything ends in death.

Unpopular Views

Schopenhauer argued that, although individuals end with death, "the essence of being is indestructible and remains part of the cosmic process." He knew such arguments would not catch on, because people find it difficult to look beyond the deaths of individuals. Schopenhauer's ideas drew widely on the philosophies of eastern religions such as Hinduism and Buddhism, which would come into greater focus in the West during the coming century.

Schopenhauer did not attract a lot of attention during his life, but he later became highly influential.

SPIRITUAL AWAKENING

In 1875, Helena Blavatsky founded the Theosophical Society to promote a new faith. Theosophy was based on the teachings of various mystics, including those from Eastern traditions such as Hinduism and Buddhism. Blavatsky's writings explained that followers could come to perceive a truth at the heart of existence, which she named the Absolute.

Among theosophical beliefs were that its followers could enter a supernatural world of spirits. Blavatsky herself claimed to be able to communicate with the dead. She also taught that the soul is reborn after death. Karma enables the soul to get closer to enlightenment in each reincarnation.

Helena Blavatsky was a Russian living in the United States when she founded the Theosophical Society in New York City.

Slow Process

Unlike other believers in reincarnation, Blavatsky said that reincarnation did not happen for some time after a person died. The soul passes first to an astral body that survives in a state of limbo before it also dies. The soul then moves into a heavenly state called devachan.

Devachan is a mental body, in which the soul remains for 1,000 to 1,500 years before it is reborn. Theosophists believe that human souls are always reborn in human bodies, instead of in those of other animals.

Wide Influence

Madame Blavatsky, as she was known, died in 1891. The Theosophical Society split over points of belief, but under the leadership of Annie Besant, one of its groups reached its greatest popularity during the late 1920s.

Theosophical teachings were highly influential. The teachings introduced people in the West for the first time to some of the ideas of Eastern religions, including the idea of karma in reincarnation, the idea that the goal of existence was to achieve freedom from suffering by attaining the Absolute, and the idea that religious experience was based upon perception instead of sacred texts and study. This led many people to explore Eastern religions more widely.

The Golden Dawn

In 1887, the Hermetic Order of the Golden Dawn was founded in London to promote magic and the occult, and paranormal activity. It taught a form of personal spiritual development based on esoteric, or elite, philosophy and forms of magic such as tarot cards, astrology, and astral travel, or out-of-body experiences. The works of members of the order such as the Irish poet William Butler Yeats helped make Eastern ideas about reincarnation more widely known in Great Britain.

William Butler Yeats carried out many magic experiments as part of his interest in the occult.

CHAPTER 5
NEAR-DEATH EXPERIENCES

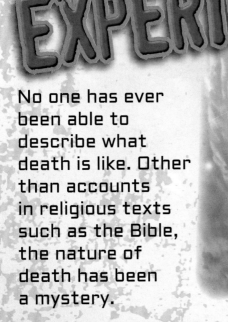

No one has ever been able to describe what death is like. Other than accounts in religious texts such as the Bible, the nature of death has been a mystery.

People who have been close to death often describe passing along a tunnel of light such as this.

In the late 1900s, researchers began to take a scientific approach to what happens to the soul after death. They wanted to establish whether reincarnation was possible, or whether ghosts existed. Reseachers began to record near-death experiences (NDE). In these accounts, a person has come close to death for a time before recovering—and remembering what happened after they "died."

Tunnel of Light

More than 3 percent of Americans claim to have had an NDE. Some of these individuals report seeing a glimpse of the "other side," which they believe is an indication of what happens after death. Many describe the sensation of passing down a tunnel of light that leads them to a peaceful place.

In some accounts, the person meets dead relatives and friends. Sometimes, the dead tell the person that they are not expected yet and must return to the world of the living. Virtually all those who report NDEs say that the experience is very calm and pleasant. Many say that their experiences have made them no longer afraid of death.

NDE Pioneer

In the early 1900s, an American named Edgar Cayce claimed to have had more than 1,400 NDEs after a first brush with death, which occurred when he nearly drowned in a fishing hole as a young boy. Cayce learned to put himself into trances, during which, he wrote, "I see myself as a tiny dot out of my physical body, which lies inert [still] before me." Cayce described following a path of light that led him past a nightmare place full of deformed humans to a peaceful place of color and music. Eventually he ended up in a vast hall, where an old man looked after records of everyone who has ever lived. These so-called Akashic Records are also known as the Book of Life.

Some NDEs involve meeting friends and relatives who have died.

A Medical Explanation?

Many doctors deny that NDEs give a glimpse of death. One study showed that more than half of people who claimed to have an NDE were not in danger of dying. Doctors say the sensation of being dead can be a trick played by the brain, as happens with a condition named Cotard syndrome. The tunnel of light might be caused by a lack of oxygen, which causes the brain to shut down from the outside.

LEAVING THE BODY

One of the best known NDEs was that of a woman from Arizona named Pam Reynolds, who "died" on the operating table in 1991. Reynolds reported leaving her body. Although some people find her account of her experience convincing evidence of life after death, others suggest it has a rational explanation.

Reynolds was suffering from a weak blood vessel near the stem of her brain. Doctors decided that they had to lower her temperature so that her breathing and heartbeat stopped. The blood would then be drained from the brain, and the operation carried out. Reynolds was given very little chance of survival, but after a seven-hour operation, she recovered fully.

Pam Reynolds was deliberately put into a state of clinical death before an operation was performed on her brain.

Special Experience

Reynolds reported that, during the operation, she heard a sound that pulled her out of her body through the top of her head. She floated above the operating room, watching the surgeons and nurses working on her body below. She said that her senses were heightened, so she could see what was happening and listen to conversations between the medics. Some of the details she observed were later confirmed as true by the medical team.

At one stage, Reynolds felt a presence in the room and was drawn toward a light, where she eventually made out the shapes of human figures. Reynolds recognized her grandmother and an uncle, among other dead relatives. She said she enjoyed their company so much that she ignored their reminders that she must go back into her body. Eventually, she says her uncle pushed her into her body, which she said was a little like jumping into a cold pool.

Proof or Not?

Reynolds' is one of the most studied cases of NDE. To some people, it is proof that there is an afterlife, which is a parallel dimension where the souls of the dead continue to exist. To those who reject NDEs, however, the story can be explained without any supernatural dimension. They say Reynolds' "memories" of the operation were in fact based on what was happening around her in the operating room after the surgery, when she was coming around under anesthetic. The white light and meeting her family, these skeptics claim, are the result of ideas Reynolds had subconsciously gathered from stories in the media and popular culture of what happens during an NDE.

This photograph creates the illusion of a spirit leaving a body. Did Pam Reynolds' story prove it could really happen?

VISIONS OF THE FUTURE

In 1984, Ned Dougherty was a Florida nightclub owner and businessman who liked to party. That all changed when he had an NDE after suffering a heart attack during a fist fight. Dougherty's NDE gave him visions of Earth's future that made him dedicate himself to a life of faith and charity.

Dougherty's book about his experience, *Fast Lane to Heaven*, describes how he met a friend who had died in the Vietnam War in the 1960s, Dan McCampbell. Communicating telepathically, or by thought, McCampbell explains that Dougherty must remember what he is about to be shown.

Ned Dougherty had a vision of a huge tidal wave washing along the East Coast through Long Island, New York City, and Miami Beach.

Meeting Mary

Next, Dougherty feels that God is filling him with universal knowledge. He is taken in a ball of light to a huge amphitheater full of spirits, where he meets many of his dead friends and relatives. From there, Dougherty goes to a marble hall, which he says was like buildings in ancient Egypt. There he meets a "Lady of Light," whom he says may be the Virgin Mary, standing next to a large globe on which flashes of lightning mark trouble spots in the Middle East. She tells him that humankind must unite to ensure that it avoids the disasters she will show him.

Future Disasters

The woman shows Dougherty a series of disasters. They include terrorist attacks on New York City and Washington, DC, which came true on September 11, 2001. She also shows him how the Earth will tilt on its axis, causing earthquakes, volcanic eruptions, and other natural disasters. Dougherty also learns that China will become the most powerful military power on the planet, and that the government of the United States will grow so weak that it will let China take power.

Since his NDE, Dougherty says that he continues to receive messages from the Lady of Light and other spiritual guides, concerning threats to peace on Earth. Critics of Dougherty say that his predictions are so general that they could mean anything at all.

Visions of Attack

A number of people reported NDEs connected with the terrorist attacks of September 11, 2001. One was Dannion Brinkley, whose NDE in 1975 left him open to visions of the future. Just 10 days before the 9/11 attacks, he predicted that the world was facing "a spiritual awakening that calls for self examination." To some people, this later sounded like a warning of the attacks. The day after the attacks, a woman named P. M. H. Atwater claimed to have an NDE in which she saw the souls of the victims forming a wave shaped like an outstretched hand as they journeyed into the sky.

CHAPTER 6

INTO THE MODERN AGE

In the late 1800s and early 1900s, psychologists such as Sigmund Freud began to study the human brain closely. Freud came to the conclusion that the human mind has hidden layers, which he called the unconscious or the subconscious. This part of the mind contains memories we have forgotten. Freud felt it was possible to learn the contents of the subconscious through careful analysis.

Sigmund Freud believed that the mind obscured people's understanding of their own subconscious thoughts.

Under Hypnosis

People began to take a close interest in the subconscious, and whether the memories it held were somehow more of a "true" reflection of a person's personalities, desires, and fears than his or her conscious thoughts. This led to a rise in hypnosis, which is a technique used to try to switch off the active parts of the brain. Some researchers saw the technique as a possible way to probe people's subconscious for any evidence of memories of previous incarnations. This method is known as regression hypnosis.

Shared Consciousness

The twentieth-century psychiatrist Carl Jung was a pioneer in understanding how the brain works. He also believed the human mind had many layers, some of which were hidden even from the individuals themselves. Jung argued, however, that everyone shared a "collective unconscious," which was a common group of feelings and instincts that were somehow part of everyone's experience.

In 1944, Jung had a near-death experience after a heart attack in Switzerland. He felt that he rose high above Earth, from where he looked back at the planet from a position somewhere above Sri Lanka, in the Indian Ocean. Jung felt that he then entered a large stone building, where he took on some kind of essential or primal form that was contained within his personality. Later, messengers from Earth told him he must return to his physical body.

Jung interpreted his NDE as a demonstration that all individuals contain some kind of "higher self," which he said in earlier times might be called god. He argued that he had had a glimpse of a realm that lay just beyond that of the living that contained some kind of spiritual meaning.

Jung's description of Earth was similar to that revealed more than 20 years later by photographs taken from space.

BACK TO THE ANCIENT WORLD

What seems like remarkable evidence for reincarnation is when people claim to be able to remember past lives. Although these memories are usually hidden, some people claim to be able to reveal them using methods such as hypnosis to reveal memories trapped in their subconscious.

Joan Grant claimed to have lived as a number of ancient Egyptians, including a princess such as the one shown in this ancient carving.

A Princess

Englishwoman Joan Grant was noted among her friends for having psychic abilities from a young age. In 1937, at the age of 20, she published a successful novel entitled *Winged Pharaoh* about ancient Egypt. The book was praised for its convincing detail, but Grant said that she had dictated it while she was in a trance-like state. She said the book was based on memories of a previous life as a woman named Sekeeta, a daughter of an Egyptian pharaoh.

In all, Grant claimed to have been reincarnated about 40 times, in various periods. She used her memories of these lives to write novels about ancient Egypt and Greece. She called the technique of recalling her previous lives "far memory," and believed it was a special gift she had learned during 10 years' training in an Egyptian temple.

Arthur Flowerdew recognized TV pictures of a city carved into red cliffs from his visions.

The Stone City

Another Briton, Arthur Flowerdew, began to experience visions as a teenager in the early 1920s of a stone city carved into a cliff. The visions lasted for years before, as an adult, he happened to see a TV documentary about Petra in Jordan, which was a key trading city that was at its peak in the first century CE. Flowerdew immediately recognized the city. He contacted the broadcaster and convinced them not only that he had once lived in Petra —but also that he had been murdered there. Flowerdew described his visions to an expert on Petra, who was struck by the accuracy of his knowledge. When Flowerdew visited Petra, he impressed experts by knowing details about the city they said could not be explained in any rational way.

A Rational Explanation

For their supporters, Grant and Flowerdew possess knowledge they have no way of learning from their normal lives. Others, however, believe they were both repeating information they had absorbed without realizing it. They may have picked up ideas from magazines, TV shows, or movies, and imagined their own versions of the past.

37

LIFE DURING WARTIME

Connecticut fire chief Jeffrey Keene became convinced that he was a reincarnation of civil war general John B. Gordon not through regression hypnosis but through a series of parallel events that awakened memories of his previous life.

A Fateful Visit

In May 1991, Jeffrey Keene visited Sharpsburg in Maryland. The town was the site of the Civil War battle of Antietam. While visiting part of the battlefield known as the Sunken Road, Keene was overwhelmed with grief that left him feeling drained, as if he had just completed a marathon.

The Battle of Antietam was fought near Sharpsburg on September 17, 1862. More than 23,000 men died during the intense fighting.

About 18 months later, Keene was looking through a magazine about Antietam when he was struck by a photograph of Confederate general John B. Gordon. Gordon looked exactly like Keene himself. In addition, Keene learned that Gordon had been killed in fighting at the Sunken Road in Antietam.

Striking Parallels

That was the first of a number of parallels Keene discovered between himself and Gordon. Keene had birthmarks on his face where Gordon had been injured. There were similarities between Keene's and Gordon's writing and leadership styles. Keene became convinced that he was the reincarnation of Gordon. He convinced others, too, by identifying objects associated with Gordon.

Keene's case is typical, say people who believe in reincarnation. His face, his personality, even the way he stood with his arms crossed, were all carried over from his previous life. Disbelievers say these are coincidences and that people who claim to remember previous lives are, in fact, drawing on their own hidden memories based on books or other sources.

I Am Anne Frank!

The Swedish writer Barbro Karlén was born in 1954, and published her first book of poetry at age 12. As a young girl, she believed she was living two lives—and that her name was Anne. When her parents took her to Amsterdam in the Netherlands, she led them straight to the house where Anne Frank hid with her family during World War II. She also identified details about the interior of the flat that seemingly only Anne could have known. The writer of the famous diary died in a concentration camp in 1945. Now Barbro Karlén is convinced she is Anne Frank's reincarnation.

A CELEBRATED CASE

In 1952, Colorado housewife Virginia Tighe visited a hypnotist named Morey Bernstein. Bernstein used a technique known as hypnotic regression, in which he put Tighe into a trance and guided her through her life in stages back to childhood. Bernstein asked another question about what came before childhood—and suddenly found himself talking to an Irish woman named Bridey Murphy. It appeared that he had guided Tighe back to a previous life.

Irish Girlhood

Bridey said she had been born in Cork in Ireland in 1798, where she lived in a wooden house called The Meadows. At age 17 she married a barrister and moved with him to Belfast, where he worked at Queen's University. She described her journey from Cork to Belfast, and gave details about her church in Belfast and even where she bought food. She told Bernstein that she died in 1864 after a fall, then left her body and experienced her own funeral. Then she had been reborn—as Virginia Tighe in 1923.

Virginia Tighe seemed to be able to describe the Irish coastline in great detail despite never having traveled there.

Fact Checking

Bernstein published Tighe's story in 1956 as *The Search for Bridey Murphy*. The book was a bestseller, and "Bridey" became a celebrity. She became the subject of a number of songs, as well as a movie. Her popularity attracted attention, however, and reporters began checking details of her story. Some seemed accurate, but others were clearly false. For example, Queen's University had not been founded when Bridey claimed her husband worked there. There were few wooden houses anywhere in Ireland, where most buildings were stone, and none called The Meadows. There were no records of the birth or death of anyone named Bridey Murphy that matched the story. In the end, even Virginia Tighe herself said she was unconvinced by the theory that she had lived before.

This photograph shows Belfast in the late 1800s, about a decade after the apparent death of Bridey Murphy.

False Memory

Experts concluded that the details Virginia Tighe revealed about Bridey Murphy's life were the result of false memory, which doctors call cryptomnesia. They say that hypnosis allowed Tighe to remember details she had forgotten about her own childhood. Tighe was adopted, but her birth parents had Irish blood, so she may have heard stories about life in Ireland. An Irish neighbor near her childhood home may also have told her stories of Ireland. That neighbor's name was Bridie Murphy Corkell.

CELEBRITY REINCARNATION

By the late 1900s and early 2000s, it had become relatively common for people to use hypnosis to explore their personalities—and the possibility that they had lived before. Some claims about reincarnation involved celebrities. Such stories have been taken seriously by some people, but less so by others.

George S. Patton, a US general in World War II, claimed to have lived as a soldier many times before.

The Spanish painter Salvador Dalí, one of the most famous artists of the twentieth century, was a Surrealist. The Surrealists tried to let loose the power of the unconscious mind. Dalí's paintings often looked as if they were conjured from his dreams. Dalí was born in 1904, almost exactly nine months after the death of his two-year-old brother, who was also named Salvador. Dalí's parents convinced him that he was a reincarnation of his brother.

Reborn Warrior

During World War II (1939–1945), General George S. Patton led US tanks into Germany. Patton believed he had been a soldier in eight previous lives. He said he had been a Roman legionary and had fought in the Turkish Muslim army. He claimed to know his way around European cities because he had fought there in the Hundred Years' War of the 1300s and 1400s.

A Buddhist Monk

The actor Steven Seagal is best known for appearing in Hollywood action movies. Before he became a movie star, he was a martial arts champion. This got him interested in Eastern faiths, and he became a Buddhist. In 1997, a high-ranking Buddhist lama, or priest, announced that Seagal was a "*tulku*," a Buddhist spirit who guided others to enlightenment. Seagal was a reincarnation of a lama from the 1600s named Chungdrag Dorje. Some skeptics pointed out that the actor had made a large donation to a Buddhist monastery before he was declared a tulku.

Hero of the Alamo

Another story concerns the British musician Phil Collins. For much of his life, Collins has been interested in the siege of the Alamo in San Antonio, Texas, in 1836, where the Texian defenders had all been killed. Collins became a leading collector of Alamo artifacts. Eventually, he met a psychic who convinced him that he was the reincarnation of a Texian scout named John William Smith. Smith had been inside the Alamo but left to carry messages before the end of the siege. Collins decided to virtually give up music to spend time investigating his links with the Alamo. It seems that the idea that reincarnation might be true remains as fascinating in the modern world as it was in the past.

This sculpture celebrates the Texian heroes of the Alamo, who withstood the Mexican army for 13 days.

TIMELINE

814 — Charlemagne, the Holy Roman Emperor, dies. Some people believe he still waits to help his people in times of trouble.

c.1136 — Geoffrey of Monmouth writes down the story of King Arthur, claiming the king still lives on the mysterious Isle of Avalon.

1208 — The Catholic Church begins a crusade against the Cathars of southern France and northern Italy, who believe in reincarnation.

1411 — Gedun Drupa becomes the first of what Tibetan Buddhists believe is a series of fourteen reincarnated Dalai Lamas.

1794 — Antoine Lavoisier attempts to communicate with an assistant after Lavoisier's head has been cut off.

1830s — Writer Ralph Waldo Emerson brings together the Transcendentalists. These American thinkers study Eastern religious ideas, including reincarnation.

1875 — Helena Blavatsky founds the Theosophical Society, which promotes a belief in reincarnation.

1887 — The Hermetic Order of the Golden Dawn is set up to investigate mystical philosophy, including reincarnation.

1915 — Sigmund Freud describes the importance of the subconscious in the mind. Some people claim the subconscious holds memories of past lives.

1937 — Joan Grant writes the novel *Winged Pharaoh*, which she says is based on her memories of life as an Egyptian princess.

1944 — Pyschologist Carl Jung has a vision of the world during an NDE.

1952 — Under hypnosis, US housewife Virginia Tighe recalls details of an earlier life as an Irish woman named Bridey Murphy.

1984 — Florida businessman Ned Dougherty has an NDE in which he is shown various disasters that will occur in the future.

1991 — Pam Reynolds describes leaving her body during surgery. Her case becomes one of the best-known and most-studied NDEs.

1997 — Movie star Steven Seagal is declared a *tulku*, a reincarnation of a Buddhist priest of the 1600s.

2001 — A number of people claim to have NDEs predicting the terrorist attacks of 9/11 in the United States.

2006 — Musician Phil Collins becomes convinced he is the reincarnation of a defender of the Alamo Mission in 1836.

GLOSSARY

afterlife A place where people continue to exist after death.

amphitheater A bowl-shaped arena.

analytical Precisely studying facts.

anesthetic A substance that reduces sensitivity to pain.

Antichrist A figure predicted to battle with Christ at the end of the world.

aristocrat A member of the nobility.

astral Non-physical.

astrology The prediction of events on Earth by studying bodies in the sky.

candidate Someone who might earn a position or job.

chemist Someone who studies substances and materials.

cosmic Related to the universe.

enlightenment Full understanding.

essence The key part of something.

funeral A ceremony to dispose of a dead body.

ghosts Spirits of the dead that remain on Earth.

hermetic Relating to ancient traditions of magic.

hypnosis A method of switching off the conscious part of the mind.

immortal Living forever.

influence An effect on something.

Judgment Day In Christian teaching, the end of the universe when God will judge all humans.

legionary A Roman foot soldier.

liberate To set free.

massacred Killed in large numbers.

medium A person who claims to be able to communicate with the dead.

mental Related to the mind.

mummies Bodies that are preserved by being dried out.

mystics People who try to understand truths about the universe through spiritualism instead of reason.

occult Mystical and magical powers.

paranormal Things that cannot be explained by reason.

perceive To observe and understand.

perception An understanding of events.

physical Existing in a solid or real form.

psychic Having supernatural powers that are not explained by reason.

quests Long, dangerous tasks.

rational Explained by reason.

resistance A force that opposes a takeover.

rituals Ceremonies based on precise actions carried out in a certain order.

sin An evil or punishable act.

skeptics People who doubt something that cannot be proved.

soul The spiritual part of a human, in contrast to the physical body.

spiritual Related to the soul.

successors People who follow someone in a particular role.

supernatural Not explained by science or the laws of nature.

Texian An early citizen of Texas.

trance A dream-like state.

visions Seeing something as if in a trance or dream.

FOR FURTHER READING

BOOKS

Green, Carl R., and William R. Sanford. *Discovering Past Lives* (Investigating the Unknown). Berkeley Heights, NJ: Enslow Publishing Inc., 2011.

Rau, Dana Meachen. *Who Is the Dalai Lama?* (Who Was?). New York, NY: Penguin Workshop, 2018.

Stone, Adam. *Near-Death Experiences* (The Unexplained). Minneapolis, MN: Bellwether Media, 2010.

Troupe, Thomas Kingsley. *Extreme Near-Death Stories* (That's Just Spooky!). Mankato, MN: Black Rabbit Books, 2018.

WEBSITES

Cathars—*www.britannica.com/topic/Cathari*
Read about the Cathars and the Church's crusade against them.

History of Reincarnation—*people.howstuffworks.com /reincarnation1.htm*
Discover the story of the belief in reincarnation in Hindusim, Buddhism, and the West.

Theosophy—*www.blavatskytrust.org.uk/html/wr_ whattheosophyis.htm*
Learn about the beliefs of Theosophy, including reincarnation.